J. R. L. AND

Illustrated by Graham Humphreys

Explorer 14   Puffin Books

Contents

1 The Vikings Burst into History 3
2 The Pirate Days 6
3 In the East 15
4 About Boats and Skis and Sledges 19
5 Home from the Sea 29
6 The Empire-Builders and After 43

Puffin Books: a Division of Penguin Books Ltd,
Harmondsworth, Middlesex, England
Penguin Books Inc., 7110 Ambassador Road,
Baltimore, Maryland 21207, U.S.A.
Penguin Books Australia Ltd, Ringwood,
Victoria, Australia
Penguin Books Canada Ltd,
41 Steelcase Road West, Markham, Ontario, Canada

First published 1974

Text copyright © J. R. L. Anderson, 1974
Illustrations copyright © Graham Humphreys, 1974

Made and printed in Great Britain by
Westerham Press Ltd, Westerham, Kent

Set in Monophoto Plantin

This book is sold subject to the condition
that it shall not, by way of trade or otherwise, be lent,
re-sold, hired out, or otherwise circulated without
the publisher's prior consent in any form
of binding or cover other than that in which it is
published and without a similar condition
including this condition being imposed on the
subsequent purchaser.

1 The Vikings Burst into History

On a June day in the year 793 the monks of the great monastery of Lindisfarne (Holy Island) off the coast of Northumberland were startled to see a small fleet of strange black ships making for their beach. The monks had little time left to wonder what this meant, for a few hours later most of them were dead. The strangers landed, attacked at once, pillaged the famous church founded by St Aidan and grown great under St Cuthbert, carried its treasures to their boats and sailed away.

That was not quite the first recorded Viking raid on Britain, for there had been a skirmish on the south coast four years earlier (in 789). But the Lindisfarne raid, with its murder of unarmed monks and wrecking of a famous church, sent a wave of horror throughout Christendom. 'Never before has such terror appeared,' wrote Alcuin of York, a minister at the court of King Charlemagne.

The Name 'Viking'

Scholars differ about the meaning of the name 'Viking'. The ending '-*ing*' is common to Old Norse and Anglo-Saxon (Old English) to denote a people or folk, and is to be found in many English place-names (**Reading**, 'the place of Reada's people'; **Barking**, 'the place of Beric's people'). Some hold that 'Viking' was used by the Anglo-Saxons before it was used in Scandinavia, and is therefore really an Anglo-Saxon word. If so, the 'Vik' part probably comes from an Old English word for 'camp', and 'Viking' would mean 'the people of the camp', a reasonable name for settled Anglo-Saxons to give to bands of raiding warriors. But the Anglo-Saxon theory may be wrong: it may derive simply from the fact that the Anglo-Saxons wrote more than the Northmen, and that more of their records have come down to us. If 'Viking' is really a Norse word, the 'Vik' bit probably comes from a word meaning 'fjord' or 'inlet', which would make the Vikings appropriately enough 'the folk of the fjords'.

A valiant monk faces the Viking horde

The terror was repeated. Two years later – in 795 – the great monastery of Iona, the mother church of Lindisfarne, was pillaged, and soon every village on the coasts of Britain and northern France began to live in fear of these raiders from the sea who came out of the north. In many churches a verse was added to the Litany – 'From the raging of the Northmen, Good Lord deliver us.' It was a prayer said fervently, and with reason.

The raid on Lindisfarne and the similar attacks which followed it were dreadful deeds, and they gave the Northmen, Norsemen, or Vikings, as they soon came to be called, a bad name. They were pagans then, worshipping Odin and Thor and other dark gods of the north, and naturally all Christians regarded them as enemies. And the Christians wrote most of the books. The Vikings have suffered from this in history, for they themselves wrote little, and most of what we know about them comes from their enemies. Pirates, robbers and killers they certainly were, though even their enemies had to admire their courage. But they were very much more than this. Archaeology and deeper study of history show them to have been one of the most fertilizing forces of the Middle Ages. In some three centuries after they burst bloodily into history with the sack of Lindisfarne they opened the Baltic Sea and the north Atlantic Ocean to trade with all the rest of the known world as far as China, discovered America, established kingdoms in Normandy and Britain, and played a large part in founding the state of European Russia. Wherever they settled they brought strong government, based on loyalty to a chieftain but embodying the idea of law-making by an assembly of the people which has developed into the parliamentary system. At a time when women in the Mediterranean world were regarded as possessions, Viking women enjoyed rights which women generally have had to wait until this century to regain. Once the Vikings had been converted to Christianity, as they mostly were by the end of the tenth century, they became stalwart defenders of the faith. European civilization owes much to them.

Who were they? Some time about ten to twelve thousand years ago, after the last severe ice age, when the climate of the northern hemisphere began gradually to improve, there was a considerable movement of peoples out of western Asia into Europe. Some of these wandering folk became particularly expert at crossing, and using, rivers. They made their way across the continent until they reached what is now north Germany and Denmark. Here, along the lower reaches of the Oder and Elbe rivers, and in what was then a marshy area of Denmark, they found conditions that suited them well, providing plenty of scope for the fishing, hunting and longshore life at which they had become expert. These were still a prehistoric people, known to archaeologists as the Maglemosians (from the Danish for 'great marsh'). People of this fair-haired Maglemosian stock spread gradually into Scandinavia – they were the ancestors of Danish, Norwegian and Swedish Vikings, as well as of the Angles, Saxons and Jutes who raided and settled in England before the Vikings came. That the Anglo-Saxons and the Vikings were people of fundamentally similar stock had an important bearing on later English history, making it easier for conquerors and conquered to assimilate after the Norman ('Northmen' = Vikings) conquest in 1066.

The Vikings we know most about in western Europe and North America came from Denmark and Norway, but their close cousins, the Vikings of Sweden, were just as brave and enterprising. They navigated the great rivers of Russia, reached the Black Sea and the Caspian Sea, and travelled far into Asia, opening the trade routes by which the silks and luxuries of the East reached northern and north-western Europe. These eastern or Swedish Vikings were widely called 'Rus', a word which gives its name to modern Russia. They were also known by the Greeks of Byzantium (Constantinople, modern Istanbul) as the 'Varannoi' (English form, 'Varangians') a name which became famous in the Varangian Guard, recruited from the Vikings to form the personal bodyguard of the Byzantine emperors. The Varangian Guard was one of the earliest of the foreign legions which have played such a notable and romantic part in military history. The courage of the Varangians was legendary, and of even more importance to the emperors was their absolute loyalty. The Byzantine court was riddled by intrigues, and there were nearly always plotters eager to seize power if they could. Unlike the Praetorian Guard of the later Roman Empire, which became hopelessly corrupt in taking bribes to make and unmake emperors, the Vikings of the Varangian Guard stood simply by their oath of loyalty and gave their lives if need be to protect those they served.

2 The Pirate Days

The Vikings were a powerful influence in Europe from about the end of the eighth century until the beginning of the twelfth, when, for various reasons and partly because of the strong and stable kingdoms that they themselves established, their influence declined. In the first century of Viking power, roughly from 800–

900, they were mostly raiders and pirates. You have to be careful about words here, for attitudes to raiding and piracy have changed over the centuries. In the ancient world, and well into the Middle Ages, the distinction between honest trade and piracy was often thin – an armed trader took what he could get by strength, paid for it if he had to. The Greek hero Odysseus regarded the sacking of a city as a proper way of restoring his fortunes, and he was admired rather than condemned for his piratical success. It was a rough age, and men fought for themselves. Nevertheless, a Viking raid was a horrible affair. The raiders sought two main forms of loot – treasure and slaves. They killed to take treasure, and when they spared lives it was to capture fit men, women and children who could be sold as slaves, for slavery was still a recognized institution then, and there was a brisk market in slaves. (The slave market in English Bristol was not stopped until a Christian bishop put an end to it after the Norman Conquest.)

Various explanations have been suggested for the sudden bursting-out of Vikings from Scandinavia towards the close of the eighth century, but the most obvious is surely right – there were

Decorative sword handles

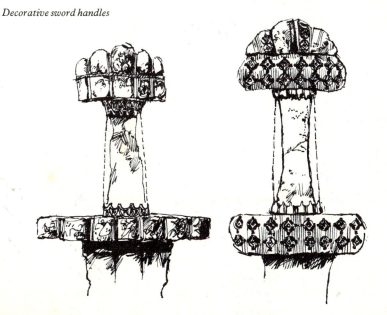

too many people for the land to be able to support them. It had happened before – the invasion of England by Angles, Saxons and Jutes in the fifth to eighth centuries took care of the growth in population up to then, but by the end of the eighth century there came what we would call another population explosion. The Northmen were a virile people, whose women bore many children. They practised the barbarous ancient custom of exposing unwanted or weakling children to die at birth, but whether many children were in fact so exposed one cannot say. Anyway, it did not do much to keep down the population, and the practice may have had another effect in ensuring that the new mouths to be fed in each generation belonged to bodies that were vigorous and strong. This may have contributed to the extraordinary toughness (and quarrelsomeness) of the raiders who set out to plunder whatever they could.

Their first aim was simply loot – the women stayed at home to look after the farmsteads along the shores of Denmark, Norway and Sweden, and the men went off raiding. It was not long, however, before the raiders began to look for more than loot and slaves to carry away – they began to seek land where they and their families could settle.

We use the term 'Viking' for the Northmen generally, whether they came from Denmark, Norway or Sweden, and the early raiding parties no doubt became considerably mixed up – the survivors of one group would join another, raid together for a time, and then disperse. There were no clear frontiers then; kingdoms expanded or shrank as individual chieftains came and went. Sometimes what is now Denmark was ruled (more or less) from Norway, sometimes it was the other way round. The eastern Vikings, who became the Swedes, seem to have been the best organized in those early days. Their kingdom of Uppland (the country around the present Uppsala) was a powerful state. These Swedes (to use their modern name) adventured mostly to the East. Danish and Norwegian Vikings (often intermingled) turned mainly to Britain, the north Atlantic islands and along the Channel coasts of Belgium and France. As time went on the Danes and Norwegians came to have more or less regular areas of expansion – the Danes in eastern

facing page: *At first the Vikings came for loot and slaves to carry away*

and southern England, Flanders and France, the Norwegians in Scotland, Iceland, the Faroe Islands, Orkney, Shetland and the Hebrides. Often they fought each other. Danish and Norwegian Vikings both raided in Ireland, and the native Irish showed considerable skill in playing off one against the other.

Pirates or settlers, by the end of the ninth century Viking raiders had made lasting marks on the map of north-west Europe. They did not exactly discover Iceland and the Faroes, because Irish monks, making wonderful voyages in their skin-covered boats called curraghs, got there before the Vikings to establish hermits' cells in those then remote places. But the Vikings came to settle as farmers and fishermen. They were not yet Christian, and the unarmed Irish monks could offer no resistance. Orkney, the Faroes and Iceland soon became flourishing Viking homelands, for long periods more or less independent. Much of Scotland was ruled from what became the great earldom of Orkney. An early settler in Iceland, Ingolf Arnason, gave the name Reykjavik to the settlement that became and is still the capital of Iceland – the name means 'bay of smoke', and Arnason called it that from the steam that rose perpetually from the hot springs to be found there. From Iceland the Vikings established colonies in Greenland, and from there the Icelander Leif Eiriksson discovered North America (which he called Vinland) nearly five centuries before Columbus sailed.

Danish Vikings made a great raid on the Thames estuary about the year 835. They encamped on the marshy islands of Sheppey and Thanet, and for the next twenty years or so they raided over much of south-east England, pillaging both London and Canterbury. Ethelwulf (father of King Alfred), who ruled over the west Saxon kingdom of Wessex from 839–58, organized a tough resistance to the raiders, gradually making it difficult for them to go inland from the Thames. So instead they turned north, into East Anglia and Yorkshire. They stormed York in 866 and then turned south again into the Midlands (then the Kingdom of Mercia). Nottingham fell to them in 869 and then, enriched and strengthened by the booty of Yorkshire and the Midlands, they again attempted to invade Wessex.

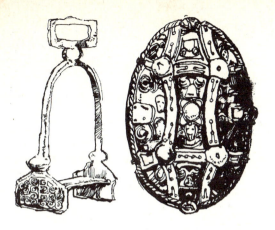

A highly decorated stirrup and a tortoiseshell brooch

Ethelwulf's son Ethelred (d. 871) and Alfred (later justly called 'the Great'), who ruled Wessex from 871–99, fought back and finally won, Alfred and his West Saxons defeating the Danish host at the battle of Edington in Wiltshire in 878. Alfred made the Viking chieftain, Guthrum, accept Christianity, and sent him packing back to East Anglia, which had become a Viking stronghold. But Guthrum had lost a battle, not a war. He and his followers were so strongly entrenched in north-eastern, eastern and midland England that in 886 King Alfred made a treaty with him, recognizing the north, the eastern counties and the midland areas of Nottingham, Derby and Leicester as places of Viking settlement, subject to Viking law (the 'Danelaw'). You will find many names of Viking origin still in use in these areas, notably place-names ending in '–by', a Norse word meaning farm (Grimsby, 'Grim's farm') or '–thorpe', meaning settlement or hamlet (Milnethorpe, 'the hamlet with a mill').

King Alfred's victory over the Vikings in 878 had important consequences in France. Learning of Guthrum's defeat, the leaders of a Viking fleet which had sailed from Denmark to the Thames to join him decided to go instead to France, where they raided profitably and savagely for several years. One result of this was that Normandy was so overrun by the Vikings that early in the next century (911) the Danish Viking Rollo (great-great-great-grandfather of William the Conqueror) was recognized as duke of

overleaf: *King Alfred's defeat of Guthrum the Dane in 878*

Normandy by the king of France. In return, Duke Rollo undertook to keep out any more Viking invaders, which he did so successfully that he made Normandy a stable, independent duchy, the first stable Viking state in western Europe outside Scandinavia.

Viking raids on France and Britain left the most permanent marks on western Europe, but those fierce, magnificent seamen from the north adventured much farther afield, too. About the middle of the ninth century Viking ships were seen off the coasts of Spain and Portugal. Lisbon, Cadiz and Seville were all attacked and pillaged. The Vikings also raided in Morocco, southern France and Italy. There, about the year 860, occurred an incident typical of Viking resource and savagery. Coasting along the Gulf of Genoa, a Viking band, led by a man called Hasting, came to a town that they thought was Rome. They were a bit out in their geography, for they had got nothing like far enough south, and the town they actually came to was a place then called Luna, near the town now called La Spezia. The Mediterranean world was new to them, and Luna looked big and rich enough for what they imagined Rome to be like. Anyway, it seemed worth looting, so they made a plot. They sent messengers, looking very humble and downcast, into Luna to say that Hasting had just died, and that he had become a Christian on his deathbed; could he, please, have a Christian burial? The bishop of Luna was touched by their story, and agreed. During the funeral service Hasting jumped from his

Looting scene

coffin and struck down the bishop. The mourners drew swords from underneath their cloaks, fell on the bewildered congregation, and looted the town.

3 In the East

While Danish and Norwegian Vikings were raiding in the west, the Swedes or eastern Vikings were making adventurous journeys in the East. One must begin this chapter with a warning. Archaeological evidence leaves no doubt of Viking penetration far into Russia, in the great cities of Novgorod and Kiev, and along the rivers Volga and Dnieper to the Caspian and the Black Sea. But the evidence can be interpreted in different ways. Most western students of the Vikings hold that the Swedish Vikings, called 'Rus', not only traded into Russia but established 'Khaganates' or kingdoms around Novgorod and Kiev, later combined, which were the foundation of the European Russian state. Certainly the name Russia seems to derive from the Rus. Soviet historians, however, consider that the Vikings were only merchant-venturers, or sometimes mercenary soldiers serving under Slav leaders, and that the Rus were a tribe of northern Slavs rather than Vikings. We are not here concerned with the politics, but with the certainly real Viking expeditions into Russia.

Like the Viking expeditions in the west, these eastern journeys were also made in boats, but here it was river voyaging, with all the difficulties of rapids, shallows and strong currents instead of ocean storms. Some rapids are so rocky and dangerous that no boat can live through them. When they came to a place like this the Vikings had to take their boats out of the water and manhandle them overland to the next navigable stretch of river. This is now called 'portaging', a word that comes into English from the French settlers in Canada, who made immense river journeys by canoe and had sometimes to carry their canoes overland. The Vikings had

15

ancestral skill as river-boatmen; a thousand years before the great rivers of North America were being used as trade routes, they had learned to navigate the rivers of eastern Europe.

That river skill took the eastern Vikings back towards Asia, but now as organized trading bands. They established an important settlement (confirmed by archaeology) at a place called Staraya Ladoga (Old Ladoga) just south of Lake Ladoga, and about 100 miles to the east of modern Leningrad. From Lake Ladoga they had a network of river systems to use. They could take the River Volkhov to Novgorod, and then, by crossing Lake Ilmen, continue south along the River Lovat to come within striking distance of the Dnieper and the Volga. Relatively short journeys overland would take them to either of these great rivers, whence they could continue along the Dnieper to Kiev and the Black Sea, or go eastwards along the Volga. Alternatively, they could go eastwards from Lake

A Viking portage around the rapids

Ladoga along the River Svir to another big lake called Onega, and thence by other rivers and lakes to join the Volga in the region of Rybinsk (on the modern map). Their river boats – or some of them – were, perhaps, built to be taken to pieces for carrying overland; and they had other boats guarded and kept ready at their main river-stations. An account of one such station, on the Volga, has come down to us from an Arab traveller called Ibn Fadlan who, about the year 920, was sent by the caliph of Baghdad as ambassador to the ruler of the Bulgars, a powerful tribe who controlled the country round the Volga bend at Kazan. Ibn Fadlan says that the Vikings had big wooden houses on the river bank where they could bring their boats alongside, and here they would live together, ten or twenty of them to a house. They made a great deal of money from trade, and their wives wore quantities of rich jewellery – every woman also carried a knife, which she wore suspended from

a ring pinned to her bosom. Ibn Fadlan was not impressed by the Vikings' personal habits, which he considered filthy, but he regarded them as the finest-looking people he had ever met.

At such trading posts as that described by Ibn Fadlan these Swedish Vikings sold what they had brought from the north – furs, amber, honey and slaves – and bought silk, spices and other luxuries from the East. There were trade routes both north and south of the Caspian Sea by which they could either go themselves to the great markets of central Asia, or meet merchants bringing goods from India and China. An astonishing relic of this early eastern trade with north-west Europe is a bronze statuette of Buddha, of Indian workmanship dating from the sixth or seventh century, which was found during archaeological excavation at Helgö, a little island in Lake Malar, near Stockholm. The extent of Viking trade with the East is proved by the large numbers of Arab coins found in similar excavations in Scandinavia.

The river-route along the Dnieper to Kiev went on to the Black Sea, and early in their history the Vikings crossed this sea, or coasted along its shores, to reach Byzantium or Constantinople (Istanbul). By the middle of the tenth century Viking merchants were such regular visitors to Constantinople that a district of the city became recognized as the Viking quarter, and they were given a charter conferring various rights and privileges. Some Vikings joined the Imperial Army, and they proved such splendid soldiers that a Viking regiment was formed, known as the Varangian Guard (see chapter 1). This became the personal bodyguard of the emperors. The Emperor Constantine Porphyrogenitus (r. 912–59) wrote a book about his empire for the guidance of his son (later the Emperor Romanus II) and in this he describes how the Vikings brought their boats down the Dnieper. He explains how they dealt with the various rapids they had to pass, unloading their boats and manhandling them overland to get round the dangerous shoals. Several of these rapids still have Viking names. At home in Sweden memorial stones were often erected to Vikings who died abroad. Several have been found commemorating men who died in Constantinople, and there are references to a mysterious 'Serkland' (literally, 'Silk-land') which refers, perhaps, to Baghdad or some

Rune Stone
'Ulf had taken three gelds in England. The first was that which Tosti paid. Then Thorkel (the Tall) paid. Then Cnut paid.'

other great market of the East where silk was to be bought. One Viking visitor to Athens carved a runic inscription (see chapter 5) on the neck of a stone lion, found centuries later in the harbour at Piraeus and taken to Venice. Unfortunately the inscription is now so worn that nobody can read it.

Many Viking names have acquired Russian forms and passed into common use in Russia: Oleg comes from Helgi, Igor from Yngvar, Vladimir from Valdemar, for instance.

Whether the early Russian khaganates or kingdoms of Novgorod and Kiev were actually ruled by Vikings or maintained by Viking soldiers recruited as mercenaries, they were powerful enough by the year 839 to be sending ambassadors to Constantinople, and by early in the next century there were formal diplomatic treaties between them and the Byzantine emperor. The great Danish scholar, Johannes Brondsted, has pointed out that in these treaties there are several Scandinavian names.

4 About Boats and Skis and Sledges

The Vikings came into history by sea, and they were the finest navigators of the Middle Ages. But they were great travellers by river and land as well as by sea, and the skis and sledges they developed for making winter journeys were often as useful as their boats.

The great black longship, or rowing warship, is, however, the picture that comes to mind first in any thoughts about the Vikings. We know about some of the boats and ships they used because of their custom of burying great chieftains with their ships, and in some cases the clay around the graves has preserved the shape and timbers of the buried ships. Ship-burial was not exclusively Viking – it was also practised by the early Anglo-Saxons, and doubtless by other maritime peoples. Like the richly furnished tombs of the pharaohs in Egypt, it embodies the age-old belief that it might be somehow helpful to the dead to surround them with the tools and treasures that had served them in life. A poor man might be buried with his sword or spade, a woman with a bit of her spindle, or perhaps a comb. Only the heirs of the very rich and great could afford to strip themselves of valuable possessions in order to furnish graves, but there are examples in many parts of the world of communities which seem almost to have beggared themselves to show piety and respect for their dead. The ship-

The Gokstad ship with a cross-section to show its construction

burial of a Viking chieftain was an enormous labour, as well as a great sacrifice of wealth, but his heirs and followers considered it their duty to do their best for him in death. One of the most famous of these ship-burials, which tells us very much about Viking ships, was found (in 1880) in the grave-mound of a warrior-chieftain at Gokstad, on the western side of the Oslo fjord in Norway. The ship in this grave – the Gokstad ship – was a great ship by any standards, 76 feet (22.3 m) long, with a beam of 17 feet 6 inches (5.25 m), and, for sheer beauty, she must have been one of the loveliest vessels that ever put to sea. She could carry between 250 and 300 armed men, a formidable fighting force.

Like almost all Viking vessels, the Gokstad ship is clinker-built, that is, with side planks that overlap each other. The planks are held together by iron rivets, and lashed to the ship's frames by tough, springy fibres from the roots of spruce – an immensely strong form of construction, and also flexible, enabling a hull to give gently to

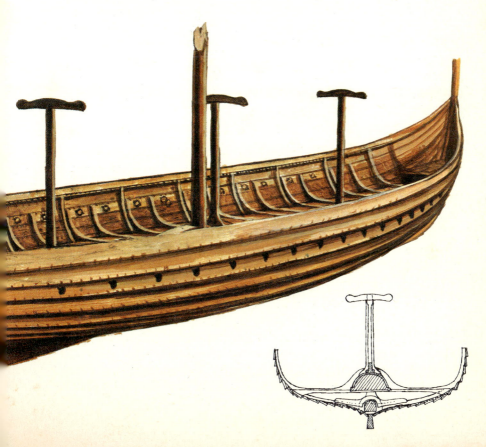

the sea instead of resisting rigidly, and so risking greater damage in rough weather. The Gokstad ship had a mast about 40 feet (12 m) tall, but it was not a permanent mast which had to be kept standing always. It was fitted (stepped) in a strong mast-block or wooden housing, so constructed that the mast could be unstepped and taken down fairly easily. This might have been useful for manoeuvring close inshore or going up an estuary, and it might have been useful, too, when men wanted to land quickly to fight on a beach. But the mast was no ornament – it carried a big square sail on a spar about 36 feet (11 m) long, to give tremendous drive when sailing. The Gokstad ship also had ports for sixteen pairs of oars (thirty-two rowers), but her oars would not normally have been used at sea. They were the equivalent of a modern sailing boat's auxiliary engine, to make her easier to manoeuvre in confined waters. The oar-ports could be closed to prevent water from slopping through them when they were not in use. Following what seems to have been standard Viking practice, the rudder was in the form of a steering oar, hung to starboard of the stern. (We get the word 'starboard' from the Vikings – the 'steerboard', or 'steering side' of a ship.) A replica of the Gokstad ship was sailed across the Atlantic by Captain Magnus Andersen in 1893. He reported that she handled beautifully, and could reach eleven knots – a good speed for a modern ocean-racer.

The Gokstad ship dates from about the year 900, and it was ships of her type that took the raiding Vikings of the tenth century to Britain, France, Spain and the Mediterranean. Clearly, however, the Gokstad ship represents the perfection of generations of shipbuilding experiment – we do not know precisely when Viking seamen discovered that sail was far more useful than oars at sea. There is some evidence that the earlier Vikings went to sea with oars. A beautiful vessel, dating from rather before the period of Viking expansion, was found at Nydam in south Jutland, and she has no provision for a mast. Nor had the great ship (of around the year 650) found buried with an Anglo-Saxon chieftain at Sutton Hoo, in Suffolk. The Anglo-Saxons, who in a sense were pre-Viking Vikings, seem to have rowed across the North Sea to raid and settle in England. But it must be remembered that archaeological evidence, depending on chance finds of what has been preserved, is very incomplete. I find it hard to believe that men bred to the sea, as even the earliest Vikings were, did not know how to use the wind by rigging sails of some sort.

The ships that have come to light in the graves of kings and warriors are naturally the kind of ship they took to sea to raid and fight from. We know much less about the trading vessels used by Viking merchants. We do know, from references in the sagas, long stories learned by heart and handed down by word of mouth, that their trading ships were capable of long voyages – to Greenland and America – and that they could carry live cattle as well as cargoes of trade goods. Here, for instance, is how the Greenland Saga describes the preparations for a voyage to America (Vinland) by the Norwegian-Icelandic Viking Karlsefni early in the eleventh century: 'He gathered a company of sixty men and five women. He made an agreement with his crew that everyone should share equally in whatever profits the expedition might yield. They took livestock of all kinds, for they intended to make a permanent settlement there if possible.' And when they arrived in Vinland: 'The livestock were put out to grass, and soon the male beasts became very frisky and difficult to manage. They had brought a bull with them.' (*Graenlendinga Saga*, translated by Magnus Magnusson and Hermann Palsson, Penguin Books, 1965.)

This indicates substantial ships, of good seagoing qualities, for only a vessel of considerable size could transport cattle, and all the

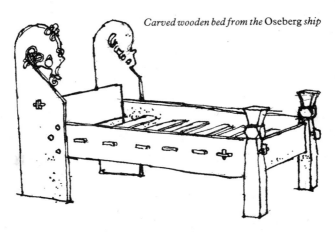

Carved wooden bed from the Oseberg *ship*

food and water needed for them, across the north Atlantic. From the remains of one or two wrecks that have come to light, from pictures on rocks, and from the development of cargo vessels in the later medieval period, we can form a fair idea of what these Viking trading ships were like. They were rounder and wider than the longships, and built for sail, not oars – they would be too heavy for rowing in the ordinary way, though they could perhaps be manoeuvred slowly by the use of long sweeps, or towed for entering or leaving harbour by men rowing in smaller boats. Unlike the warships, built for carrying men rather than cargo, the merchant ships were fully decked, with a big hold amidships. The crews of the longships would normally try to put into some beach to sleep ashore; if they had to make long passages they would huddle under skins or makeshift tents to rest. The much smaller crews of the merchant ships (probably no more than twelve) could make themselves snug below deck. There might not be room to stand up, except in the hold, but they could spread their bedding in some cubby-hole with protection from the worst of the weather. The fighting men lived at sea on such cold rations as they could carry, but the merchant seamen could cook on a brazier in a sand-box (burning on sand to lessen the risk of fire). We know too, again from the sagas, that women and sometimes children made long voyages as passengers on these ships.

The Vikings were among the earliest of the Volga boatmen. Their river-boats had to carry slaves and as much merchandise as possible. Going downstream, a few rowers could give them steerage-way, and a skilful helmsman would keep them bow-on to the current, leaving the current to do most of the work. Upstream meant a hard slog at the oars or towing from the bank, though sometimes on the great rivers of Russia it would be possible to sail. Navigating rapids or shallows was gruelling work. Sometimes a boat could be taken through light, which meant unloading all her cargo, carrying it round the bad stretch of river, and loading up again in clear water. Where it was too dangerous for a boat to be taken through, the boat as well as the cargo would have to be dragged overland. The boats might be hauled on rollers made from tree trunks, or they could be taken to pieces and re-assembled.

facing page: *A Viking trading ship carrying goods and horses*

The Vikings had neither compass nor sextant – yet they were able to make, and return from, long ocean voyages. This demanded skill and experience, but other seamen of the ancient world were equally able to make long voyages, and the navigation of the Polynesian islanders in the Pacific has shown what seamen are capable of without anything in the way of instruments. The sun and the stars have taught men to distinguish north, south, east and west from the earliest times, and the Vikings – as we still do – sub-divided the sectors between these cardinal points into north-north-east, north-east, east-north-east, etc. Given the sun or the stars to steer by, you can always follow at least a rough course. But on long voyages there are overcast days and nights. Then you are liable to get lost, but if you keep your head, and have sea-room, the sun will come out again, or the Pole Star re-appear at night. We know from the sagas that the Vikings took observations on the sun. The Greenland Saga tells us of the Viking Bjarni, trying to sail from Iceland to Greenland about the year 980: 'The fair wind failed, and northerly winds and fog set in, and for many days they had no idea what their course was. After that they saw the sun again, and were able to get their bearings.' (Magnusson and Palsson.)

We don't know precisely how they did it, but we do know that they did. There are many possible ways. The farther south you get (in the northern hemisphere) the more nearly the sun is directly overhead at noon – i.e., the shorter the shadow cast by the sun at noon. You can make a fair guess at noon by watching the shadow of a stick shorten until it begins to lengthen again, and you can measure or estimate the length of the shortest shadow, and compare it with the noon-shadow of the place you started from, or where you want to go. It is possible to measure sun or star-angles roughly with a notched stick. By such means you can get a rough idea of whether you are north or south of the place you are heading for – in modern terms, you can get a rough idea of your latitude (though the Vikings didn't know the word). It may be a very rough idea, but it will be a great deal better than nothing, and at least you will know whether to head north or south. You can't know where you are in an east-west direction (longitude) because you haven't got a chronometer, or even a watch – it was not until late in the

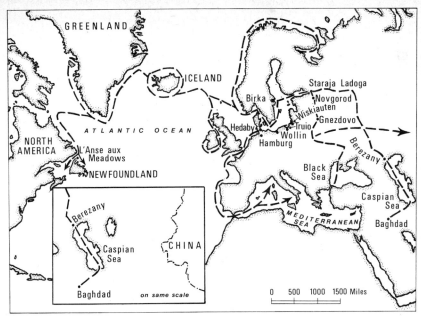

The Vikings ranged widely from the East Coast of America to the borders of China

eighteenth century, nearly 900 years after the Vikings discovered America, that men had any practical means of reckoning longitude at sea. But you have kept your head, and you can guess. You know the feel of an east wind and a west wind, and as a good seaman you have been noting changes in the direction and strength of the wind all the time. So you act on such knowledge as you have – the feel of the wind, the run of the waves, the look of the sea and the sky – and you steer as you think right. Sometimes you will be badly wrong, and your ship and your crew may never be heard of again. But you have been at sea since boyhood, and often you will have guessed reasonably well, and after some anxious days and nights you will sight land. The North Sea and the north Atlantic, where the Vikings sailed, are rough waters, but there are no desperately long passages between landfalls. It is less than 400 miles from Norway to Scotland, and there are all the islands of the Orkneys, the Shetlands and the Hebrides to provide the mariner with landfalls. Between Norway and Iceland lie the Faroes, and across the

27

Denmark Strait from Iceland is the great mass of Greenland. It is an unattractive and dangerous coast, but it can help to tell the sailor where he is. On rounding Cape Farewell at the southern tip of Greenland, a passage of 700 miles will sight Newfoundland, and then there are coastal landmarks for passages northwards to Labrador, Baffin Island and back to the west coast of Greenland and southwards to all the eastern seaboard of Canada and the United States, where the Vikings found the land they called Vinland. (The Viking voyages to Vinland are described in the Explorer *The Discovery of America*.)

Seafaring and sea-raiding are the best-known aspects of Viking history, but these tough people were also great travellers by land. Over rough country with few roads it was easiest to travel in winter, and the Vikings had well-made, efficient sledges, horse-drawn, or pulled by teams of men. They had an ingenious form of horseshoe, with iron spikes, which they fitted to their horses' hooves to give a good grip on ice. They used skates, sometimes made from bone, and their forbears invented skis, the most efficient form of travelling over snow ever devised.

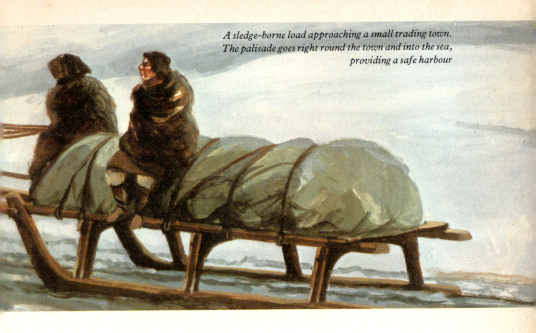

A sledge-borne load approaching a small trading town. The palisade goes right round the town and into the sea, providing a safe harbour

5 Home from the Sea

The Vikings were farmers and fishermen as well as pirates and raiders – the same man would often be all of them in turn. The typical Viking settlement was a farm, but a farm that had to be self-supporting; clothes and sails (for Viking sails were frequently made of wool) came from the farmer's own sheep, the wool spun and woven by the women. Weapons and tools had to be made on the spot (though there were travelling smiths for the more skilled metal work), food had to be dried and salted to last the winter. The commonest Viking home was a long hut – 50–80 feet (15–24 m) long – with raised platforms down each side on which people slept: sleeping places were marked off by rows of stones. In the middle of the hut was an open fireplace, for burning wood or peat. There were no windows, though in the bigger huts there might be openings in the walls, with shutters. There was no glass for ordinary people then, although an ingenious man might make a semi-transparent sheet out of a pig's bladder and fix it to an opening to let in a bit of light, but this was rare.

In well-forested Scandinavia there is plenty of wood and houses were mostly built of wood. There were several styles – log cabins, the gaps between the logs filled in with clay, a lattice-work of twigs between load-bearing posts plastered with mud that dried hard (wattle-and-daub), 'stave houses', built of planks standing upright, like barrel-staves. In Iceland and the Atlantic islands (Faroes, Orkneys, Shetlands) there is very little wood, and houses were built of stones, roofed and covered with turf. Driftwood brought by the sea was collected and guarded carefully, for boat-building or for roof beams.

The basic Viking crops were barley and oats, which, pounded into meal, were made into porridge or rough bread. For rations at sea, the grain would be roasted, or parched. This is not very nice (to my taste, at any rate) but roasted grain will keep at sea (to be made into a sort of bannock) whereas fresh flour will mildew and go green quickly. The small Viking fields – tiny by modern standards – were scratched from hillsides, and ploughed with great labour by the *ard*. This, the standard Viking plough, was basically a crooked stick, sharpened to a point, and (if there was a blacksmith handy) sometimes reinforced with iron. The *ard* was held and guided by one man (by a woman, if her man was away raiding at sea), and pulled either by another man, or by an ox. Some experts say that the richer Viking farmers also had the more efficient wheeled plough, equipped with mould-board and ploughshare, but others hold that the wheeled plough was unknown during the main period of Viking expansion. Whichever be the case, the plough used by most people was certainly the *ard*, and turning hillsides into land capable of growing crops was gruelling hard work. Farm animals included ox, goat, pig and sheep, of which the sheep, providing wool as well as meat, became by far the most important. Wool was vital to the Viking way of life; spun and woven by the women, it provided the only cloth they had, for the sails of boats as well as clothing for people, though leather was sometimes used for sails and outer garments. Linen, when there was any flax to be had, was sought eagerly: one of the attractions of raiding and settling in Britain and Ireland was that flax could be grown, and linen and canvas made from it. Linen clothing was a great luxury, and canvas sails were both more efficient and more hardwearing than sailcloth made from wool.

Keeping alive in winter was always a problem. Few animals, apart from carefully guarded breeding stock, which more or less lived with the family, could be kept through the winter, for there were no root-crops or other feeding-stuffs. A few goats or hardy sheep might be able to live out during the winter, but farm animals had mostly to be slaughtered in the autumn, and their flesh salted to provide food for as long as it would keep. In most of the Viking areas, however, there was fish, which could also be dried and salted to provide some reserve against famine. It was a world without potatoes – that wonderful crop brought from America after the voyages of Columbus was still 500 years away.

There was no sugar, and the only sweetener was honey, which could also provide mead to drink. Beer, brewed from barley, was known, and (if the records are to be believed) drunk pretty copiously. If the Vikings had spirits, not much is known about them – there is remarkably little evidence about distilling. It seems

Viking kitchen utensils

31

The inside of a typical Viking long house

hard to believe, though, that men as generally competent as the Vikings in extracting a livelihood from slender natural resources, did not extract some form of vodka, whisky or other grain spirit from the grain which they knew how to brew. Perhaps distilling was a secret so closely guarded that no one wished to say anything about it.

A Viking childhood was a tough but exhilarating experience. Many children did not survive it, but those who did grew into strong, independent men and women. The boys would start going out in fishing boats with fathers, uncles and elder brothers almost as soon as they could walk, acquiring boatmanship and seamanship as naturally as they breathed. The girls would work on the family holding, and help their mothers to spin and weave, to cook and to preserve food. Every family had to be self-sufficient, and in becoming self-sufficient they made themselves into the strong, adventurous people who could raid and settle anywhere in the then-known world.

In the earlier Viking days (and for poor people all the time) every member of a farm community lived in the same long room – the master and mistress with recognized places at one end, servants and slaves, each with his or her little pile of bedding, along the sides. As time went on, a farmer who prospered would build on to his longhouse, adding either wings in the form of an L or an E, or separate buildings. Horses, cattle and pigs seem usually to have had separate stables, byres and sties, though sometimes farm animals shared what room there was with the family. Corridors or passages seem to have been unknown in Viking houses. Basically they were one-room, and if there were two rooms you walked through one to get to the other.

The backbone of Viking society was the karl, or free peasant-farmer. He crewed the longships (Viking ships never had slave rowers) fought in raids, farmed and fished and hunted. Below him were the thralls, bondsmen or slaves, who could be bought and sold, and who had few rights. A man could be born a thrall, or he could become one, by being captured in a raid or by going bankrupt. He could be given freedom in return for some particular service to his master, or he could be ransomed, but otherwise he lived and

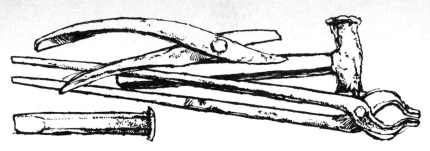

Some Viking tools

died a slave. In small communities, where everybody lived together, the lot of the thrall probably seems worse on paper than it normally was in fact. Above the karl were the chieftains and men of leading families, the jarls (earls), to whom a karl might owe allegiance. As clan-groups became more organized the jarls themselves would recognize a king, to whom everybody owed allegiance. At first kings were elected by assemblies of jarls and fighting men, but as time went on kingship tended to become hereditary (though it was often disputed). Laws were made, and upheld, by an assembly of free men, called the 'Thing', which was a form of parliament. Districts were known as 'Hundreds' (originally a hundred families) and every Hundred had its 'Thing'. On great occasions these Hundred Things came together in regional or 'national' assemblies. These Things, or parliaments, were an important check on the power of kings and jarls.

Land was inherited by eldest sons, thus providing a strong incentive for landless younger sons to go off as pirates and raiders to win fortunes and land for themselves. Women could and did own property, and free women could divorce their husbands if they wished. On divorce, any dowry that a woman had brought to her husband had to be paid back. Free Viking women were very independent. When a Viking farmer went off on a raid, his wife ran the farm as a matter of course. The sagas tell of one particularly formidable woman called Freydis who led her own expedition from Greenland to America, and murdered her rivals. This was somewhere between the years 1005 and 1015.

Viking hospitality was legendary, and no traveller was ever

turned away. Jarl's hall and karl's house were much the same sort of communal longhouse, though the jarl's would be bigger. During the long nights of the northern winter, there would be feasting round great log fires in the longhouses, flares lighting the fierce bearded faces, smoke swirling round the rafters. The master, his family and servants and any guests, would listen eagerly to heroic stories, mostly about their own ancestors, recited by the saga-tellers, who travelled around with their stories. There would be much drinking of mead or beer – the Vikings liked wine, but seldom had it, unless they had come back from a raid on France.

The Viking farm: the farmer is ploughing with an ard

One of the gifts brought to north Europe by the Swedish Vikings was the game of chess. Chess seems to have been invented in India, but no one knows when or where. It spread to Persia, and in the later Sassanian period (sixth to seventh centuries) it became very popular there: the chess term 'check-mate' derives from the Persian *shah-i mat*, meaning 'death of the king'. In their eastern journeyings the Swedish Vikings got to know of the game, and brought it home with them. It soon became popular, and good chess-players were much admired. There were doubtless some noble contests during those long northern winter nights.

The Vikings were not townsmen, or even villagers – their settlements were based on individual farmsteads, though as a farmer grew rich his farm would have more buildings to house retainers and their families, and gradually grow into a village. But trade made it necessary to have towns for markets, and there were some famous medieval market towns in the Viking homeland round the Baltic. One was Hedeby, near Schleswig on the modern map, in an area that was then Danish. It was fortified by great earthworks, and archaeologists have found traces of many industries there, including iron and bronze working, potteries, textiles, and a mint for making coins. An Arab merchant, Al-Tartushi, who visited Hedeby around the year 950 described it as being almost at the end of the world, but he was impressed by the number of wells to provide fresh water (almost every house seems to have had a well) and by the quantities of fish available for food. He was also

The main Viking trading towns

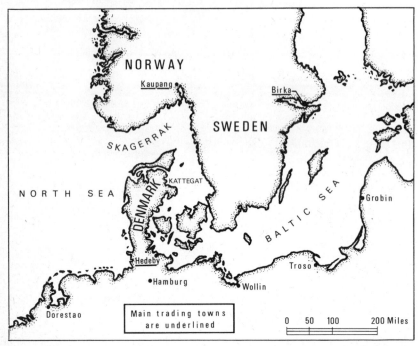

38

impressed by the independence of the women there. He was not impressed by Viking singing, which, he said, was like dogs' howling, only worse! Hedeby was sacked and destroyed by King Harold Hardrada of Norway about 1050 – the same Harold who was killed in battle against Harold of England in 1066, a few days before the English Harold was himself killed at the Battle of Hastings that won England for William of Normandy.

Another Viking town was Birka, on an island in Lake Malar, near Stockholm. This was the great market town of the Swedish Vikings, famous for its trade in furs and amber from the north, and in silks and jewellery brought by Viking merchants from the East. Birka was destroyed about the end of the tenth century, how is not known, but probably in a war between Denmark and Sweden.

For most of the period of Viking expansion the Vikings were pagan, worshipping a complex collection of gods. Some of them were shared by the pagan Anglo-Saxons, and have given us names for some of the days of the week (Wednesday = Odin's or Woden's day, Thursday = Thor's day). There were at least two distinct strands in Viking paganism, fragments of a very old nature-worship, in which Freya was a mother-goddess of fertility, and a later warrior-cult in which the chief figures were Odin and Thor. Odin was the chieftain of the gods, living in his great palace of Valhalla, surrounded by a bodyguard of warriors who had been killed in battle. Next to Odin – and more approachable by ordinary people – came Thor, a mighty fighter, wielding a gigantic hammer. Thor used his hammer mostly for destroying evil creatures, and he was regarded as a fairly kindly god, ready to help seamen and farmers with the everyday problems of life. It must be remembered that the concept of an all-merciful, all-loving God came into the world with Christianity: pagan gods and goddesses might be persuaded to help men, but they had super-human passions as well as super-human powers, and were figures of awe rather than of mercy.

Although the Vikings during their great period were mostly pagan, they were not all pagan, nor were they necessarily pagan all the time. There were Christian missions to Hedeby and Birka in the ninth century, the Viking leader Guthrum was converted by King Alfred of England, and Christianity gradually overcame the

overleaf: *A Viking trading town. The roadways were probably made of logs. Goods were also carried on the waterways*

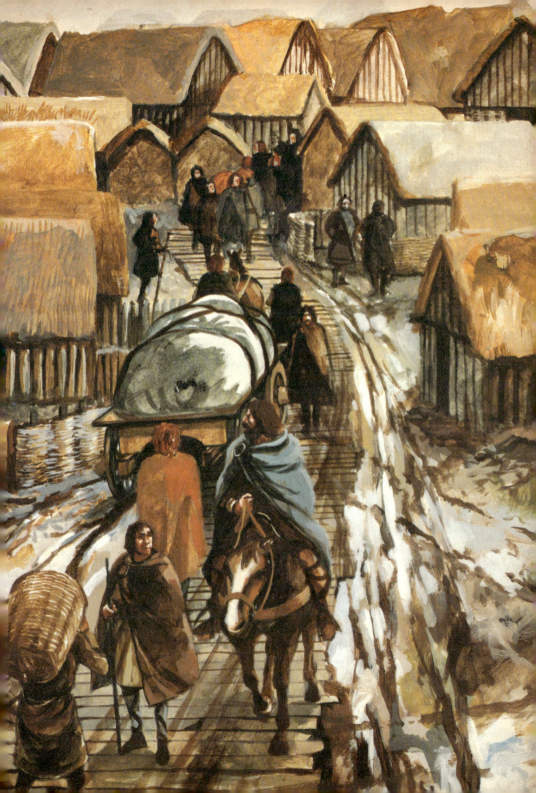

older faiths. Rollo of Normandy became a Christian in 912, a year after establishing himself as independent ruler there. Iceland adopted Christianity in the year 1000, by formal resolution of the Icelandic Thing, or parliament (there were never any kings in Iceland). In that resolution it was agreed that people might still sacrifice to the old gods, provided that they did so in private. This provision was soon afterwards withdrawn, and the Icelanders became exceptionally devout Christians.

For all their fierce behaviour, the Vikings were an imaginative, indeed poetical, people, with a strong sense of humour. They loved to give nicknames to each other, nicknames that have survived to sharpen the picture of the men and women who bore them. There is the grimness of a raiding chieftain in Erik Bloodaxe, vivid description in Harold Finehair, Svein Forkbeard, and Siward the Snake-eyed. Poetry and respect come together in Aud (a woman) the Deep-minded. Although they did not write much, the Vikings had an alphabet of their own, called (after its first letters) the 'Futhark', as we say 'A B C'. Here these first letters are:

F   U   TH   A   R   K

The letters themselves are known as 'runes', and as well as being used for writing they had a magical significance and were often inscribed on weapons or charms to bring good luck. The Anglo-Saxons also used a runic alphabet very similar to this. It goes back at least to the second century AD, and may be older still. It clearly derives from the Roman alphabet, perhaps with some direct influence from Greek (the 'th' rather suggests this). The letters, mostly straight lines and good sharp angles, seem to have been designed especially for carving on wood, and this is probably why there are so few early examples of Viking writing, because wood soon weathers and perishes. Later, runes were cut in stone, and many inscriptions on stone can still be read. Woodcarving seems to be the natural Viking art, but after they began raiding England and Ireland, stonecarving, perhaps learned there, became more widespread. They had a wonderfully decorative art, using lines and patterns in a style that we would now call 'abstract', and intertwining these patterns with the figures of strange heraldic animals. A Viking artist did not like to leave any space blank – he filled every inch with his patterns.

6 The Empire-Builders and After

In the tenth century the character of Viking raids began to change. They ceased to be hit-and-run robberies, and became determined efforts to win kingdoms. In France the Viking Rollo made Normandy an independent duchy. In England King Alfred was followed by strong and able son, grandsons and great-grandsons, who fought the Vikings to a standstill and kept them in check in the eastern and northern counties recognized as more or less settled Viking areas (the Danelaw). Then, towards the end of the century came Ethelred II (979–1016) known from his weakness and incompetence as Ethelred the Unready ('Unready' meaning here unwise, or just plain silly). He tried to buy peace by paying Viking bands to stay away, forcing the English to pay a special tax for this called the Danegeld. The Vikings took the money, and came back for more. In contrast to Ethelred, Denmark produced an exceptionally able king called Svein Forkbeard. He led raid after raid on England, exacting enormous sums in Danegeld (in 994 alone, 16,000 lb of silver) and gaining control of more and more English territory. In 1013 Ethelred, who had married the sister of the duke of Normandy (Richard II, grandfather of William the Conqueror) ran off to Normandy, and Svein was recognized as king of England. In 1014 Svein died. After a confused few years he was succeeded in 1017 by his son Cnut (Canute), later known as Cnut the Great.

Carved animal head from the Oseberg ship found in the grave of a woman chieftain, possibly a queen or princess

With the Anglo-Saxon Alfred the Great, the Viking Cnut the Great must rank among the best and wisest of medieval rulers. He was a Christian, respected and helped the Church, and set out to strengthen the rule of law everywhere. He became king of Denmark as well as of England, but he did not try to force the English to obey Danish law: he recognized Anglo-Saxon law and customs in Anglo-Saxon England. He worked to create a north Atlantic empire, uniting Scandinavia and Britain, and so successfully that, as the historian Sir Keith Feiling put it 'he was obeyed by Viking settlements from the Vistula to the Hebrides'. Had he lived, he would surely have brought Iceland and the Greenland settlements within his realm, and perhaps have understood the importance of the Viking discovery of America that came during his lifetime. But he did not live: he died at the age of thirty-nine in 1035. His sons had none of his greatness. The dream of empire vanished in feuds and squabbling.

But the Vikings were still destined to rule England. Cnut's sons Harold (r. 1035–40) and Harthacnut (r. 1040–2) had short troubled reigns, and after the death of Harthacnut (apparently of drink) the last of the Anglo-Saxon house of Alfred, Edward the Confessor, became king. Edward died childless in 1066, and although there were descendants of his half-brother Edmund Ironside, an outsider, Harold Godwinson, who had been the king's chief minister, seized the throne. The Scandinavian Vikings, however, were not prepared to lose England so easily, and Harold Hardrada, a powerful Viking chieftain who had made himself king of Norway after winning fame and riches in adventures in Constantinople and the East, attacked almost at once. Harold met and defeated him at Stamford Bridge, but in the same week the Norman Vikings, under Duke William, landed at Pevensey. Harold was killed at Hastings, and the Norman Viking William became William I of England.

Rival Viking attempts to recapture England did not end at once. In 1069 Svein Estridsson, king of Denmark, sent three of his sons and a fleet of 250 ships to the Humber, where the Viking army landed and captured York. William managed to contain them, but could not drive them away, and the next year (1070) King Svein brought reinforcements from Denmark, marched south and took much of East Anglia, including the towns of Peterborough and Ely. After this Svein allowed himself to be bought off and went home. In 1085 one of his sons, another Cnut, assembled a combined Danish and Norwegian fleet to renew the attack. That fleet never sailed, for there was a rebellion in Denmark, and Cnut was killed. After this the Normans were too strongly established in England for further invasion from Scandinavia to be contemplated.

Danelaw: the area of Viking rule in England

So the Vikings did win dominions in western Europe, in Normandy and Britain, and in large areas of Brittany and Flanders, too. Their own successes put an end to further Viking expansion: conquerors and conquered fused together into strong national states, more than capable of making history on their own. This fusion was most complete in England, where Norman Vikings and Anglo-Saxons came from common stock. In Normandy there was more division between native French and conquering Norsemen. Even so, the Viking dynasty of Rollo ruled Normandy for close on 200 years, from 911 until 1204, when Normandy was effectively abandoned by King John, great-great-grandson of that William who had added England to his domains along the Seine. And Viking blood lives on in many Norman people, and Viking speech in many Norman place-names.

In Ireland the Vikings established no lasting colonies: they warred too much among themselves, enabling the native Irish in the end to drive them out. But Dublin, Cork, Limerick and several other Irish towns were founded as Viking fortresses and remain as permanent landmarks of Norse occupation. In Scotland, especially on the north-east coast, and in the Scottish islands, many of the present inhabitants are of Viking stock, still bearing Scandinavian names. In the north Atlantic islands, Iceland and the Faroes, Viking settlements took permanent root – their people are Vikings to this day. The great Atlantic adventures from Iceland, first to Greenland, across the Davis Strait to Baffin Island, and then to what are now Newfoundland, Nova Scotia and the United States, made the European discovery of North America. It came too early in European history to be of political importance (though what might have happened had Cnut the Great lived, and had able successors, is another matter). But these Viking Atlantic voyages remain some of the greatest navigational feats of all time. An eighteenth-century king of Denmark contemplated claiming sovereignty over North America by right of Viking discovery 700 years earlier, but by then the English, the French and the Dutch were all established there, and the Danes had no hope of enforcing their claim.

In the east, the Rus or Swedish Vikings who had settled, if they did not rule, in Novgorod, Kiev and other Slav territories, gradually adopted Slav customs and embraced the form of Christianity that became the Russian Orthodox Church. They have left some graves and grave-goods, and Viking names in the Russian tongue. Influential as they certainly were, they were never more than a tiny minority among the surrounding Slav peoples, and their colonies – if, indeed, they tried to found any – could not have endured. Their long trading links with Constantinople and the East were weakened by the Crusades (First Crusade 1095) which brought western Europe into direct contact with the cities and markets of Asia Minor. Direct trade with the East via the

Mediterranean put out of business the Viking merchants and their long, laborious river journeys. The crack Viking regiment in Constantinople – the Varangian Guard – became a sort of Byzantine foreign legion: after the Norman Conquest many Englishmen who had lost their lands went out to join it. By the end of the eleventh century the great days of Viking expansion were over.

But the Viking story has not ended. Modern Danes, Norwegians, Swedes, Icelanders and Faroese embody the tough Viking spirit and tradition of lawmaking by assemblies of the people that had so great an influence a thousand years ago. Viking seamanship lives on in the fine sailors of Scandinavia, and in the seamen of many other nations, too. And the wonderful art-forms of Viking craftsmen are, perhaps, even more admired in the twentieth century than they were in the tenth.

Acknowledgements and Further Reading

In preparing this study of the Vikings I have been helped greatly by Professor Johannes Brondsted's *The Vikings* (Penguin Books) and David Wilson's *The Vikings and Their Origins* (Thames and Hudson). I also owe a particular debt to the Statens Historiska Museum, Stockholm, and to the National Maritime Museum, Greenwich, for much kindness and help during the important Viking exhibition mounted by the Swedish museum at Greenwich in 1973. Those who would like to explore farther into the fascinating world of the Vikings cannot do better than start with Professor Brondsted's and Dr Wilson's works. With this background, they will be able to turn with deeper understanding to the vivid translation of the Vinland sagas, *Graenlendinga Saga* by Magnus Magnusson and Hermann Palsson published by Penguin Books. A good starting point for exploring the Byzantine empire, in which the Vikings played such a considerable part, is *Byzantium*, a collection of studies edited by N. H. Baynes and H. St L. B. Moss (Oxford Paperbacks).